SURRENDER

RELEASE YOUR PAST, GET OUT OF YOUR OWN WAY, AND JUMP INTO YOUR FUTURE

BRADLEY CHARBONNEAU

REPOSSIBLE

PRAISE FOR EVERY SINGLE DAY

A QUICK SELECTION OF BOOK REVIEWS FROM PEOPLE WHO ARE NOT MY MOM

If you're new to my ~~work~~ play, you might like to have a quick read of what other books of mine have done to help transform the lives of readers just like you.

I hope Surrender transforms and transcends as much as "Every Single Day" did.

I especially like how "P.C." writes below "There's a **spark** within me that has been relit."

I get my inspiration and content from you and I hope to keep up that connection.

~

> "Somehow, I found myself devouring this today. It's rare that I allow myself this indulgence as the list of what I need to be doing in my head is endless.
>
> **Deliciousness to my soul**, is the description that comes to mind as I reflect on my experience of consuming this book. I have no idea how to write a review and put into words **how deeply this resonated within me.**
>
> **There's a spark within me that has been relit.** I know **ESD is the kindling I need to get the fire crackling and roaring** ... there are flames here that need to breathe and light the world.
>
> Thank you Bradley Charbonneau for accepting the challenge of ESD, so that today, you could influence my ESD."
>
> — 5 STARS FROM P.C. VIA AMAZON

~

"I love how you handle **deep subjects in such a light-hearted way.**"

— Kay Bolden

~

"**Before reading this book I was ashamed of myself.**

For years I had called myself an artist but I knew the truth. I was only masquerading as one. ... But could I continue to call myself an artist when I stoped making artwork? The answers is no.

I am not entirely sure what happened to me from the time I was in college until now, eight years later. There was **a shift that took place** in my mind during that time.

I **developed a fear** of making artwork. I would always make excuses as to why I just couldn't create. I was too tired, the dog needed a bath, I needed to do dishes. What was the point of painting anyway **because no one would want to buy or look at my work** etc.

I have spent many years working dead end jobs just to pay bills. I **never even allowed myself a chance** at having a career because I would give up at the slightest failure or rejection.

The few times I did really try, I won awards at competitions.

I now have a two-year-old son. I have used him as an **excuse** to not make art for the past two years. I **feel guilty** that I put so much blame on my son. Taking care of him was just a convenient excuse that is easily believed by most people.

After reading this book, there is no going back. I have no choice.

I make artwork everyday and I am happy. ... I know there is no going back.

I was miserable with guilt and now I am not.

I was afraid to create and now I happy to learn once more.

When I started to draw again I was really rusty but I got through it. **I find time** even though I take care of my son all day and I babysit my nephew for eight and a half hours a day.

I wrote this review in the hope that I could inspire someone else to change their life.

Take the Every Single Day challenge. Read this book it just might change your life."

— Paige

~

"The author shows us how to get past "**analysis paralysis**" to actually start projects and see them through until completion.

A theme of this book is to **dream about doing something until the dream itself is internalized along with the willingness to progress toward goal completion in iterative steps taken each day**. Readers will learn the importance of getting past inertia in order to begin complex tasks and progress toward a completion date with certainty.

Everyone who moves toward a meritorious goal must first start, stumble, reassess and move ahead with a refined approach toward reaching the goals set forth at the outset. **Very few, if any, tasks are completed with zero failure points or stumbles.** A strong point of the book is that the author sets up readers for roadblocks which must be overcome as part of the learning process. The book could be labelled alternatively as "what it takes to succeed"!"

— Dr. Joseph S. Maresca, Amazon "Hall of Fame" Reviewer

“Maybe you've let your dreams rust.

Author Bradley Charbonneau has published several children’s books and travel books, but in this ‘self-help’ genre he **unveils his own secrets for making life meaningful and successful.**

... the author opens the gates to his pathway for fulfillment and success. **‘I transformed myself when I made the decision to change my behavior.’** He places bold statements throughout to make sure he has our attention, phrases such as **‘Dreaming the dream was a whole lot easier than living the dream.’**

This fine book encourages us to take a very deep breath, start afresh, and make or lives what they CAN be. A very fine book.”

— Grady Harp, Amazon “Hall of Fame” Top 100 Reviewer

~

“This author has provided an excellent "how to" book, to **move past procrastination**, and **getting past fear**—teaching the reader how things made habitual can result in transformational success. This book could be **a really important read for the new, young person looking to "start" his life journey**, or switch directions after a rocky start. His writing is humorous, friendly, and engaging. I have bought two copies - one for both of my adult children.”

— Robert Enzenauer

~

" ... for anyone with **dreams hidden in the attic, cellar or heart.**"

— Amazon Reviewer

~

"He lights a path that you can choose to walk down."

— Ray Simon, accomplished speaker, and a no-longer-secret trumpet player

~

"A **very earnest sharing** by someone who has found his destiny and a way to achieve it."

— Bandaluse

❀ Created with Vellum

PREFACE

A PREFACE IS WRITTEN BY THE AUTHOR AND TELLS READERS HOW AND WHY THE BOOK CAME INTO BEING.

Had anyone told me even a few short years ago that I was going to be writing a book called *Surrender*, I would have laughed, then shrugged it off, taken another sip of my brew, turned around to talk about something else, and maybe not ever thought about it again.

Then my dad got cancer.

I didn't know what to do but I knew I wanted to help. I *needed* to help.

I read so much you'd think I was doing a Ph.D. thesis on cancer.

I stumbled onto special diets, I wade my way through drugs and medicines and even medicine men in Peru. Blueberries, celery juice, trips to Brazil. Maybe hallucinogenic drugs, maybe tapping, possibly hypnosis. No, I know! Everything at the same time.

Whew.

I read, I listened, I studied.

I tried to be patient. I struggled. I cried. I gave up. I started again. I thought I was helping. I knew I was helping. Was I helping?

I doubted, I feared, I kept going.

I practiced, I tried, I learned.

One of the books I read was called Radical Remission. It was written by a conservative doctor who was baffled by all of the people who "healed" from their cancer through other means—means other than the *normal* pathways of chemo, drugs, radiation, etc. She went down a rabbit hole of research and found 9 elements of the people who had healed.

The majority of those didn't involve blueberries. The majority was in our minds, our hearts, our mindset.

I had the audiobook and would "force" my dad to listen to it in the car. He accepted it because it was written by a conservative doctor. He believed it because of the science behind her studies. He surrendered to it ... well, I'm not sure he surrendered to it.

But I did.

Then I found Joe Dispenza. Another scientist, researcher, author and man with an insatiable curiosity for the unknown, the path less traveled, and the super natural.

I started to practice meditation. I went to a day-long silent exercise with a course I was taking on mindfulness. Then a 3-day weekend workshop. A 5-day workshop where we'd wake up at 4 AM and do 3-hour meditations. I finally did a Vipassana 10-day silent meditation marathon of torture, I mean, retreat where I:

1. Think I went crazy on day 7, stole a pen from the kitchen (we weren't allowed to write!), went to the bathroom and wrote furiously on a roll of toilet paper about what I had bottled up for the past 6 days.
2. Talked to a deer in the woods.
3. Realized I didn't need to do too many more 10-day silent meditation retreats to get to *the other side*.
4. Figured out 17 minutes every morning was also good.
5. **Accepted** that there is some sort of higher power within us.
6. **Believed** I had this power—and believe that we all do.
7. **Surrendered** to it.
8. Have lived an easier, more joyful, peaceful, creative, glorious, delicious, fun, funny, silly, wild, mystic, real, real fun life ever since.

With this book, my dream is to start you on your journey or pull you along faster or take your hand and lift you up higher.

I don't know if you need to do all of those retreats although I have to say, being together in a group of others doing the same thing, all at the same time, with the same goals, sharing accountability, pain, suffering, dreams, desires, wants, needs, and anything and everything in between probably got me to where I am today a whole lot faster than I even would have made it alone.

No, I retract that.

I don't think I ever would have made it alone.

Which is one of the reasons I'm writing this book.

We do have an inner genius. I'll call "it" by many names in this book but there is "something" out there that guides us, helps us, lifts us up.

I don't really care what you call it—well, other than I'm curious and sometimes it's really funny! (See chapter where I mention Tinkerbell...)

My dream of all dreams is that you are **open** to the idea of it.

Why?

Here's my honest answer and the answer I believe from the bottom of my heart: I think it will make the world a better place.

Though each of us, individually, improving ourselves, rising up, lifting up our own selves, it's almost impossible to not lift up those around us.

Then it's just a chain reaction.

A woman I met at a conference floored me to the core once when she said something like:

> "All we need is for someone, even a stranger, to walk up to us and directly say I love you."
>
> — M.C.

Then she said:

"Here. I'll start. I love you."

— M.C.

Wow, we're only in the preface of this book and already I'm getting down and dirty, I'm tossing out the light and fluffy and digging in and getting real. Because, are you ready for this? I'm going to say something to you that I wouldn't dared even write down a few years ago yet here I am saying it you, probably a perfect stranger.

Ready for it?

This might just be the invitation you've been waiting for from an unexpected source. Maybe I am that unexpected source.

Here.

I'll start.

I love you.

Welcome to *Surrender*.

“If you knew who walked beside you at all times, on the path that you have chosen, you could never experience fear or doubt again.”

— Wayne Dyer

DEDICATION

To Joe Dispenza

He taught me not only was it OK to surrender but that beyond this was where the good stuff was.

CONTENTS

INTRODUCTION

WHAT TO EXPECT

Expect the unexpected.

This book is more than words on a page. This book, these words on pages, are one element of a plethora (I don't know how much a "plethora" really is but I just like saying that word) of media to get us from accepting to believing to surrendering.

Words on a page can only do so much (says the WRITER!).

Please come on over to surrender.repossible.com for downloadable guided meditation audio files, video enhancing topics in this book, quizzes, document downloads and who knows what else might appear in there.

Another aspect of it all is communication. Collaboration. Cooperation. Although you don't have to come join us and "get involved," it's the "involvement" that helps me, helps you, helps us get to where we're going faster, with more scenic routes, and plenty of stops for date shakes.

Read and/or listen along to this book, click on a link, come join the Surrender party happening over at Repossible Central.

I look forward to seeing you there.

- **Possible:** read

- **Impossible:** get date shakes outside of California
- **Repossible:** surrender to a larger group to boost your progress

P.S. Date Shakes. I'm not kidding about the date shakes. We used to have them somewhere in the California desert out past Palm Springs (where lots of dates grow). Even as a kid, although dates looked a little bit like fat cockroaches, the sweetness of the fruit and the sharp vanilla bean together in a cool shake was a delight incomparable under the hot sun and next to the fatigue of long drives.

PROLOGUE

In the dedication to this book, I mention that surrender is "where the good stuff is."

By "good" I mean: fun, funny, silly, powerful, angelic, magical, and the deliriously delicious foray into the glorious empire of the unknown.

You know when someone shows you their workspace and they say, "This is where the magic happens."

Surrender is where the magic happens.

FOREWORD

BY MR. LEE

You're supposed to have someone else write the forward to your book.

This book is called *Surrender*.

I'm going to write my own.

As if I were my own greater self to whom I'm surrendering.

Yeah, well. There you have it.

When my wife and I were traveling through Vietnam, oftentimes people would call me Mr. Lee.

I guess they saw my last name and then, consciously or not, thought, "Whoa, there are a whole lot of letters in there and I'm not even going to bother possibly botching that pronunciation." and they called me Mr. Lee.

Get it?

- First name: Brad
- Last name: Lee

I tried to correct them for a while but then I kind of got used to it and it was fun—and kinda funny.

One guy even asked me if I had a brother Bruce.

I know, I know, it's a country full of stand-up comedians, let me tell you.

On that same trip when we were in Zimbabwe, and this is a really long story but I'll keep it short, my wife was asked if she would like to work behind the bar of the lodge where we were staying.

Her first reaction was no.

When she told me about their request, my first reaction was also no.

In fact, it was almost:

"No, of course not."

It was a little mountain village called Chumanimani some hours outside of Harare in the country of Zimbabwe.

I know I mentioned the name of the country before but I just like saying and writing *Zimbabwe* because I can't think of a more exotic-sounding place on the planet.

So if you think about what they were asking, it was pretty crazy. To work behind the bar at a lodge in a mountain village, one called Chumanimani no less, in a country called Zimbabwe, and of course the answer must be no.

Right?

Because who does that sort of thing?

Clearly not me. Not my wife. Not us.

We just weren't the type of people who did that sort of thing.

As we talked about it more, we thought to ourselves:

> "Well, how do people become that sort of person? Who are those people who do that sort of thing? Where is the form to become that type of person and can we fill it out?"
>
> — Us, Wondering to Each Other

We were on a year-long trip around the world. We had one appointment all year: a wedding in Stellenbosch, South Africa in February. It was late November.

If you looked at it rationally:

1. We had the time
2. We had nowhere else to be
3. We had the skills (well...)
4. We were already there
5. We already knew the place
6. We had a place to stay
7. We would get free room and board

But still. When we asked ourselves, "What type of person does a thing like that?" our gut reaction was still, "Well, clearly not us."

How do you become such a person? Transform? Is there a surgical procedure? Do you have to do four years of training?

It turned out, there was no procedure to transform what type of people we were other than one simple, not always easy, step:

A Mindset Shift: Dare to Play

The only thing holding her back from taking the job was daring to say yes, taking the playful route instead of the "expected" route, accepting that it was possible, that yes, even a girl from a small town in The Netherlands could work behind a bar in a mountain village in Zimbabwe.

Because, we slowly figured out, the difference between:

- The type of person who does a thing like that

and:

- The type of person who doesn't do a thing like that

is deciding right there, on the spot, that you are, from now on, going to be the type of person who does a thing like that.

Why Us?

We wondered how it could be us when there were certainly other people who were more qualified or who had the time or who would just dare say yes and yet...wait a minute. We had all of those qualifications.

Why Not Us?

It turns out that the only difference between that other woman who was working behind the bar (and was leaving, thus the open position) and us was she had the mindset of "Why not me?" and "I'm the type of person who does a thing like this." and she said one different thing, the first word out of her mouth was not "No" but it was this other word, this powerful three-letter word that sometimes can be hard to believe is possible but it's so easy to say.

It sounds like ***guess*** but it's more powerful.

It's just a few letters away from ***less*** but it's so much more.

It's similar to ***stress*** but then that word goes away when you just say this three-letter word.

"Yes."

That was it.

That was the difference between the chosen ones, the ones who did things like that and those who didn't.

That was the shift. The **acceptance** of changing who we were, of **accepting** that it was possible, **believing** it could be us, and **surrendering** to a "higher power" that was there all along.

My wife said yes.

In an instant and right there in the mountains, we changed our personality from those people who don't do things like that to people who do things like that.

I'm pretty sure this was right around the point where, at least from my perspective, I knew this was the woman I wanted to marry.

I wanted to spend the rest of my life with a woman who "was that type of person who did this sort of thing" or even better yet, was someone who could transform, right before my eyes, from a person who didn't do that type of thing to a person who did.

Soon after, another position was open and I said that same three-letter word.

In a matter of days, **we surrendered to our present and futures and dismissed the doubts of the past.**

We ended up working at the lodge through Christmas, serving the chief of police his favorite Tusker beer, learning the hard way that a rum and Coke wasn't half rum and half Coke, and I even got to call my parents from the broken payphone outside that let me share with my family that we had become people like that who do things like this.

We surrendered to our future.

Mr. Brad Lee
Driebergen, The Netherlands
2020

- **Possible:** believe you cannot possibly be a person who does things like that
- **Impossible:** forever succumb to accepting that you're not the type of person who does a thing like that
- **Repossible:** surrendering to become the type of person who does a thing like that

PART I

ACCEPT

"The only tyrant I accept in this world is the still voice within."

— Mahatma Gandhi

1

INTRODUCTION TO ACCEPT

WE NEED TO ACKNOWLEDGE WHERE WE ARE BEFORE WE CAN MOVE FORWARD.

> "We must let go of the life we have planned, so as to accept the one that is waiting for us."
>
> — Joseph Campbell

There are (at least) two elements of Acceptance:

1. Accept where are you today.
2. Accept that there is a greater version of yourself.

Let's get into the first one because it's required to then move onto the second one and also, this first one can be quite the annoying roadblock to getting further at all.

Accept Where You Are Today

Accept where you are before you can get start leaving where you are. To get to the next level, onto the next personality, phase in your life, we first need to figure out, acknowledge, and accept where we are.

One element of this acceptance is "being OK with it." Not just, "OK, fine, I accept this is where I am even though I'm not happy about being here and I really don't want to be here and I'd rather be further along by now." but embracing, even being, grateful for where you are.

This was (and is) always a struggle for me. I find myself saying things like:

- "But I don't want to be here."
- "I should be further along by now."
- "I deserve to be at a higher level at this point."
- "Well, this sucks."Whereas the cross-legged monk in me feels like I'm supposed to be saying:
- "I thank my past self for getting me to the point where I am today so that I can move forward from here."
- "I'm grateful to be even at this point in my life for I might have been much further behind."

What if where we currently are in a cocoon stage of our lives and the next stage is when we emerge as the beautiful butterfly? Could we have, should we have skipped that boring, stupid, annoying cocoon stage? The butterfly thinks not.

But I know, I get it, I'm in the same boat (or maybe the same cocoon): I want to be the butterfly. Could we hurry up this claustrophobic cocoon stage, please?

Speaking of the butterfly...

Accept that there is a greater version of yourself

We don't have to be in the cocoon forever.

We don't have to be that slimy, segmented, truly odd beast that is a caterpillar.

We can become the butterfly. In fact, and this can be hard to grasp while we're still feeling like a caterpillar, we currently are that future butterfly we're just in another form right now.

Here we go with the part that gets a little harder to grasp if you're still feeling like the caterpillar. Yes, we are that future butterfly right now even though we don't feel like it but even better is that while we're the caterpillar, we have access to the butterfly. The butterfly's wisdom, experience, even beauty and outlook from that perspective.

Let's move away from the crawly and flying insects for a moment and come to us, to people.

What is your butterfly? Or maybe who is your butterfly? Who will you be in the future? We now, yes, right now, have access to that future self, our own future self in all of its glory, fame, fortune and whatever else we seek and strive towards.

Let's go beyond even the butterfly for a moment.

Sure, she's beautiful, brilliant, and, I mean, come on, she can FLY while we're stuck crawling on way too many legs down here on the ground.

But what if this greater being is something even greater than what we can imagine? What if there is a greater self, a larger-than-life source or entity or __________ (fill in the blank as to what you think might be there) that is accessible for us?

Allow me to guess where you're heading right now in your thoughts? Let's do a bullet list of my guesses at words that are going through your mind right now.

- God
- god
- Spirit
- Source
- Universe
- Greater self
- Angel
- Tinkerbell

Any of those pop into your mind yet?

I especially like Tinkerbell because this being, this floaty existence we're trying to "accept" here in the "accept" chapter could be anything.

Ready for the hard part?

Because up until now I'm throwing out terms we might be familiar with but maybe don't quite, well, accept.

Yep, that's it.

To get to this next level of self, to rise up, to elevate to where we want to go, we can do it quite a bit faster, easier, and with more bells and whistles when we accept that there is a greater force out there guiding us, leading us, or at least with a stick and a flag like tourist groups in Rome, available to us to tap into.

There are you have it.

That's the second part of acceptance–it's a doozy, I admit.

That there is something greater than our physical self out there, well, maybe not even so far out there, maybe it's "in here" or right next to us at all times.

- **Possible:** god
- **Impossible:** Disney
- **Repossible:** Tinkerbell

Here's a short video version of Part 1 of the 3-part process of Accepting, Believing, and Surrendering: Accept. It's over on surrender-accept.repossible.com.

2

ALL OF THOSE CATERPILLAR LEGS HOLDING ON

THE EFFORT ISN'T IN THE CLIMBING UP, IT'S IN THE LETTING GO (AND FLYING).

"Abundance is a process of letting go; that which is empty can receive."

— Bryant H. McGill

We're slogging up that branch carrying our heavy body even though we have all those legs. We're not going to fall because each little foot has a vise grip on each spot.

We're not letting go.

We're happy where we are.

We can even imagine what might come next but we know if we fall down, if we let go, we'll probably die a squishy, gooey death below.

Or a bird will swoop down and eat me.

But yeah.

You know when someone tells you to relax and you think and maybe you even say, "But I am relaxed." Here's a little test you can do.

When you think you're relaxed, clench every muscle you have control over. When you have done that, make it even stronger. Grip your teeth like you're holding onto a rope that's keeping you above water. Tighten your toes, flex your back, make muscles in your arms, fists, and even fingers.

At this point, you're probably holding your breath.

Let that breath out quickly through your mouth. If you'd like to add a little theater and you aren't in a, well, theater, give it some oomph, make some noise, let your dog know you're letting go of that breath.

As you let that breath out, unclench all of your muscles. Really let them loose. Ideally, you're sitting or lying down and not standing because if you're standing, you'll probably fall over if you're really letting it all out.

Feel how loose everything is? Your hands might dislocate from your wrists it seems like. You can even close your eyes but then let your eyelids go heavy, closing over your eyelids like a blanket over a baby at night.

Feel that?

That's the caterpillar letting go.

OK, OK, biology majors, I know the caterpillar will fall to its demise below if it doesn't go through the whole cocoon thing, but stay with me here for a minute.

For most of the day, we're holding on. It's hopefully not as tightly as the caterpillar is to not fall off the branch but it's probably pretty close.

Letting go, surrendering, is more about loosening our grip on our daily existence, our familiar thoughts, and even our unfamiliar dreams than it is any sort of strenuous action.

Remember tightening up all of our muscles? That is stress, that is strenuous, that is what we often do all day, all week, all year.

The letting go, the loosening up, the falling from the branch and then, OK, stay with me for the sake of the visual, transforming into a butterfly as we float down is surrendering.

- **Possible:** clench
- **Impossible:** stay on the branch forever
- **Repossible:** let go

3

YOU DON'T HAVE TO TELL YOUR BODY TO HEAL YOUR BROKEN ARM

YOUR BODY KNOWS WHAT TO DO

"Climate is what we expect, weather is what we get."

— Mark Twain

You break your arm. Ouch. You go to the doctor and what do they do? Put a cast on it. A simple case of plaster molded around your arm so it doesn't move much.

Then you wait for your body to fix your broken bones in a matter of weeks or months.

You didn't have to learn how bones work, what they're made of, or how your brain or heart or whatever-is-at-work-here got down to the business of pushing molecules and cells and protein together so your two broken pieces of cartilage in your body meld back together.

Who is running the show here?

Also, even if you told your body (or pleaded or hoped, prayed, or meditated) to NOT heal your arm, it would still heal your arm– although it could take longer.

So how much influence do we have over what our body can and can't do? Do we have any say in the matter at all? That bone is going to heal because your body wants what's best for you.

What about things going on that aren't working out in our bodies quite as we hoped? Disease, medical conditions, pain, allergies, etc.? Do we have any say in how those heal–or don't heal? If our bodies supposedly want what's best for us, what's up with the stuff that's wrong with us?

I've stated this clearly before but for the record and the legal hawks watching, I'm not a medical doctor. About the closest I am to a medical doctor is I used to have a white coat. I think it was a jean jacket. It was pretty bad. Yeah, sorry.

But I have more "say" about my body, how I feel, how things are going in my life, but also physical conditions than I used to. What changed? Did I get a medical download from above? Have I practiced meditation to the point where I can guide my body (and mind and thoughts and actions) more in directions that I would like it to go?

Remember the ATM? Forgetting your PIN code and then walking away and then remembering it? Just for example's sake, just in case this could be somewhere in the ballpark of truth and reality, what if we laid out our intention to ourselves, we told (or pleaded or asked) our selves if something or other could be achieved. I smell a numbered list at hand.

What if we asked ourselves to:

1. Lessen our back pain
2. Stop the allergic reactions to certain foods
3. Open our imaginations to more clarity on work projects
4. Give us goosebumps on our arms
5. Wake up earlier
6. Dream more vividly
7. Remember those dreams
8. Figure out the next chapter of our book
9. Direct our next steps in our business
10. Know what to say to our kids
11. Decrease the limp in our gait
12. Heal our tumors
13. Produce tears in our eyes

14. Smile
15. Sleep more deeply
16. Wake up more refreshed
17. Improve our eyesight

How about that #14, aye? We do have control over our bodies. When we want to smile, we can do it. On command. Without a reason. Just saying.

I hear you:

> "Bradley, seriously? You have smile, produce tears in our eyes, figure out the next chapter, and heal our tumors in the same list? You can't be serious."
>
> — Incredulous You

I have a book coming up called Play, so no, if I can help it, I'm rarely serious nor take much of anything "seriously" in the sense that we most know the word.

In all of the books in the multiple-book Repossible series, Play might be the hardest to achieve because, and this is going to sound crazy but you might get it if you're stuck in the idea of "C'mon, get serious, Bradley!" we have a hard time accepting that our higher selves are "lighter" than we are. They're fun, fun-loving, easy-going, and they're pranksters, jokers, and don't take too much at all seriously.

I am fully aware that in the past few tiny little seemingly insignificant paragraphs, I have mentioned healing tumors, smiling, seriousness, playing and even a dabble into the idea that I, yes, Bradley Charbonneau, have an idea of what our greater selves are like.

Crazy, I know.

But I'm not backing down.

Are you looking for serious? Here's serious: take it less seriously.

I'm going to go out on a limb here and dangle my reputation as a serious author (ha, joke inside of a joke...) and state that our greater selves, our higher beings, our _________ whatever you want to call them or it or her or him, are not looking for you to be too serious about all of this.

Let me try to explain what I mean by serious–and what I don't mean.

By serious, I mean trying, especially trying too hard, practicing too much, striving for perfection, and expecting too much, too soon, and all because that's "the way it's supposed to be" or maybe "that's what it said in the book."

I'm going to take it to another extreme to attempt to bring home the concept.

Say there's a baby in the room. Right next to you. Her mom left for a minute and asked if you could keep an eye on the baby for 5 minutes. What do you do?

Do you explain tax law? Do you put on your professional face and and walk through your resume and introduce yourself as Mrs. Johansson?

No. Of course not.

You might make a funny face. You might make baby sounds as best you know how. You might even get up and dance around a bit, but probably in an exaggerated fashion for the most impact.

All trying to do what, of course?

Get the baby to smile or even better, laugh.

Dear reader, this is only my humble opinion, your mileage may vary, but here I am the author of a book on surrendering with an upcoming book called Play and a previous book in the series called Meditate. I've been meditating daily for years, I've attended hard-core Vipassana 10-day silent meditation retreats, got up at four in the morning to do a marathon meditation with 400 of my closest friends in a freezing Munich hotel in December.

I'm here only as the messenger. Believe me, if I thought the goal were for us to take things more seriously, I would tell you, I would suggest trying harder, smiling less, joking never, and pressing on.

Surrendering has more to do with the baby next to you than the greatest guru on the mountaintop. No, I take that back. That guru on the mountaintop? They are the baby. They are smiling, giggling, and life is light, fun, and all they want to do is play.

Please don't take just my word for it but when you're struggling to "surrender" to your greater self and you're seemingly not making much progress, think of the baby and how you would "communicate" your message. See if you can better connect than when you're trying harder, taking it more (and more and more) seriously, and pursing your lips instead of relaxing them to their natural state of a sly smile.

Whew.

We started off this chapter by healing a broken arm and we have descended (or is it ascended...?) to the point of trying to make a baby giggle.

Yep, that's exactly where we are.

They are related. Oh so related. It's almost one and the same.

Yep, your body will take care of healing your arm. But what about that next chapter of your book? What about the clarity you're looking for on that work project? How to talk with your kids? Healing that tumor?

Surrender.

- **Possible:** take it too seriously
- **Impossible:** laugh too much
- **Repossible:** smile and wave, boys, smile and wave

4

"BASECAMP TO CONTROL CENTER: SURRENDER CONTROL. THANK YOU."

BUT WAIT, ISN'T A CONTROL CENTER SUPPOSED TO, YOU KNOW, CONTROL?

"The creative process is a process of surrender, not control."

— Julia Cameron

It's kind of annoying, especially if you like to talk and speak and generally make your voice heard, but there's a saying that says something like:

"We have two ears yet only one mouth. Listen more and talk less."

— Someone said something like this

There are artists, writers, even architects, lawyers, and musicians who will glow when they talk about getting into the *flow*.

When you have not experienced something like the "flow state" where something greater takes over your imagination or your thoughts and your pen (or keyboard or project) seems to take on a life of its own and "writes itself," then it can be really frustrating to hear about because it sounds so easy.

Here's the good news and the bad news: it is easy.

Once you get into this flow state, it's easy to create (to write, work, whatever it is you're doing).

The hard part is getting into that flow state.

We're in a book called Surrender. Three guesses for you how we're going to find that cherished flow state.

You got it!

You're so quick.

We're going to "surrender to a higher power" and let the flow state take us away.

> "Yay! Sounds so fun!
>
> So, yeah, great. Where do I sign? What pill do I pop? What magical elixir do I sip to experience this out-of-body state?"
>
> — Ohso Reddy

Remember there were easy parts and hard parts? The weird part of getting into a surrendering flow state is finding the balance.

- **Possible:** listen
- **Impossible:** create
- **Repossible:** listen then create

5

YELLING AND SCREAMING, ANGER AND REGRET

CHANNEL THAT ENERGY ELSEWHERE

"For every minute you remain angry, you give up sixty seconds of peace of mind."

— Ralph Waldo Emerson

I was out in front of my house talking with a neighbor when we heard yelling and screaming. It was that guttural, deep, "angry yell" that I associate with drunks, sociopaths, and the movies, maybe theater.

It was almost as if it were being acted out.

But it wasn't.

It was in the neighborhood. *(See below for an update.)*

Then I return to my house and record guided meditations about surrendering to a higher power, I meditate in my bathroom in darkness and my mom speaks to me and suggests directions in my life, and I'm looking for more ways to incorporate song and music into my guided meditations to bring them even more to life.

Please, dear reader, I am not a "competitive" guy. I'm much more about cooperation, collaboration, and "a rising tide lifts all ships."

I'm not *better* than the guy in the neighborhood, I don't have access to more knowledge than he does, I don't know all of the tricks of the trade.

So what's the difference?

I know some of the tricks of the trade.

Why is he yelling and screaming and I'm meditating and recording guided meditations? What would I like to tell that guy?

"Dude, chill."

But I don't know the guy very well. I don't know you, dear reader, very well, yet here I am "telling" you to, well, chill.

But chill and do what?

Chill and meditate?

Chill out and "surrender to your higher power?"

Well, yeah. That's what I'm saying.

What's the difference between you and the neighbor?

You're reading a book called "Surrender." You're open to new methods, (yet) unheard of techniques to improve ourselves, to let go of our anger, to focus that energy in a positive way rather than focusing on the negative.

Again, please. I barely know the guy. His cousin might have murdered his cat. I have no idea what's going on.

But I hear anger. I feel the regret, the passion, the fear.

How can we redirect that?

What's that Alcoholics Anonymous prayer?

> "God, grant me the serenity to accept the things I cannot change, the courage to change the things I can, and the wisdom to know the difference."
>
> — Alcoholics Anonymous

I can't change the weather outside. But I can change the "weather inside."

Do I not have things to yell and scream about because I meditate? Or is it just coincidence?

Could it be that because I create and let it out on a regular basis it doesn't build up and I don't have the need for a huge outburst?

Is it possible I not only survive but thrive on feedback from people I reach, people like you, who benefit from information and experience I share, who write to me and let me know I helped them —helped you?

I'm searching for anger. I don't have much.

If I had to dig some up, I would be "angry" that people are angry and spend their time yelling where there are such better methods to let it out.

> ***DISCLAIMER:*** *Who am I to say all this? What do I know? Maybe it's his version of meditation! Maybe he's a Zen master and he's practicing for an acting part in the local theater! Maybe I know nothing and I'm just guessing, I'm assuming. Yep, maybe.*

One of the books in the Repossible series is called Dare. As I type these words, as I dare to pen this chapter, I'm fully aware this might sound judgmental. However, in my experience, it's a chapter like this where I'm not sure I should hit publish that hits home with (some!) readers and they are thankful I dared publish it. Then I am thankful that I dared publish it because it helped you, it reached out to you.

As I put together this book (and keep adding bonus content to the Meditate book), I am recording guided meditations. I'll make sure to create one for anger.

OK, in between that last paragraph and this one, I did it.

I'm on a roll, I created one for anger. You can find it at surrender-anger.repossible.com.

- **Possible:** listen
- **Impossible:** yell and scream forever

- **Repossible:** accept, believe, and surrender to your higher self

Follow-up: in case you were worried, another neighbor happened to come home and she knows them better and she contacted the wife to check in and see that all was OK.

PART II

BELIEVE

"Faith is to believe what you do not see; the reward of this faith is to see what you believe."

— Saint Augustine

6

INTRODUCTION TO BELIEVE

AND YOU THOUGHT "ACCEPT" WAS HARD…

"We cannot solve our problems with the same thinking we used when we created them."

— Albert Einstein

It's a bit of a huge leap to go from not accepting to accepting. From accepting to believing can be an even bigger jump.

If accepting is the caterpillar thinking that it's possible for such a beast to transform into an elegant, colorful, flying beauty, then believing is the point where that same caterpillar realizes it's possible for her.

There's pretty much only one thing that separates the "accepters" from the "believers" and that's experience.

Personal, real, repeatable experience.

In other words, our friendly caterpillar can read books all day, watch videos, take courses, and even hear it direct from butterfly friends but until she experiences it herself, it's going to be a tough sell.

Here's the difference:

1. I think it's possible (accept).
2. I think it's possible for me (believe).

We've gone from the safe world of theory, "Well, I suppose the world could be flat..." to the side of personal experience where you've been in an airplane, looked out the window, and saw the curvature of the earth.

Enough with caterpillars and airplanes for a moment.

Concrete Example: Writing

Before I stared writing, I accepted that one could be a writer. I didn't really believe it was possible for me because, well, uh, yeah, I didn't really have any good reasoning as to why I shouldn't believe it (but I had plenty of bad reasons: self doubt, fear, etc.) but I also didn't have personal experience as to why I could actually become a writer myself.

Until I, duh, started writing.

I added the "duh" in there just to annoy myself and make me regret (even more) how I spent years not writing yet only dreaming of it.

I accepted that it was possible for others.

I didn't believe it was possible for me.

The caterpillar accepts turning into a butterfly is possible but when it comes to her? Seriously, this fat, slow crawling blog of goo? How in the world?

Yet one day, it happens.

Then she goes from accepting to believing.

I only started believing I could become a writer when I started writing.

So simple.

So hard.

So potentially frustrating.

Yet so rewarding once we get past each level.

Imagine how much fun it's going to be to get to surrender.

Bit Harder to Grasp Example

You break your arm. You go to the doctor, get a cast.

All the doctor is doing is adding this bunch of hardened plaster so your arm doesn't bend.

What's happening behind the scenes is that your arm is healing. The broken bones, somehow, meld back together and after a certain amount of weeks, your arm is probably as good as new.

You accept his happens because you know about it, it's just common knowledge. But now you believe it because it happened to you.

Are you ready to surrender to it?

- **Possible:** break your arm
- **Impossible:** heal your arm yourself
- **Repossible:** let yourself heal your arm—and believe in it

Ready for the visual? A video interpretation of believe is over on surrender-believe.repossible.com.

7

CREATE TO SURRENDER AND SURRENDER TO CREATE

YES, IT SEEMS CONTRADICTORY. IT'S NOT.

> "Waiting around for inspiration is like waiting for the grass to grow. You know it's happening but you can't see it. Then you get bored and leave."
>
> — Mr. Brad Lee

We quoted Julia Cameron in the chapter on "the surrendering process" and it's even more relevant because she is the author of "The Artist's Way."

Back when I was a budding author (READ: depressed, frustrated, drowning in sorrow...), I used Julia Cameron's The Morning Pages on a daily basis.

> "Morning Pages are three pages of longhand, stream of consciousness writing, done first thing in the morning. *There is no wrong way to do Morning Pages*– they are not high art. They are not even "writing." They are about anything and everything that crosses your mind– and they are for your eyes only. Morning Pages provoke, clarify, comfort, cajole, prioritize and synchronize the day at hand. Do not over-think Morning Pages: just put three

pages of anything on the page...and then do three more pages tomorrow."

— JULIA CAMERON

I could have spent those mornings waiting around for inspiration to strike, quietly hoping to "surrender" to my greater power so my pen would magically take over my hand and write brilliant prose.

- So I wrote.
- Then wrote some more.
- Finally, I wrote a bit more.

While I was busy writing, I was subconsciously "surrendering" to a greater self.

Oops, did you catch that?

I was creating, writing, making, doing, keeping busy by moving my fingers over the keyboard and taking action.

Then—and only then—can I surrender to a higher power because then—and only then—have I created something of a direction towards which I would like some help from that higher self.

Through creating, writing, doing, I got the wheels in motion, I got myself into action, and then the surrendering part can kick in.

Let's stick with trains.

Because I left the station (started writing—or started whatever it is you're working towards), I put the train in motion.

The surrendering process then swoops down onto the moving train and pushes it along. It makes the train faster, it lightens the load, it might even change the tracks slightly.

But surrendering is not going to get the train out of the station. For that, you need to create, to ask, dare, spark, start, try, fail, give it a go, and go in any direction you think you should.

It's as if surrendering is waiting above, even just slightly above, for movement and once it sees any action, it can help. But it can't help when you don't help yourself.

But I Just Want to Sit Around and Wait

I get it. It seems easier.

But that would be something like waiting for the train to leave the station and yet you don't know which direction it's going in.

Sure, that might be fun but chances are high it's going in a direction you don't want to go.

Let's be clear: this is fine. Go for it. Take the ride, enjoy the trip. If it's your path, keep going.

But learn from it, turn around if you'd like, and then get the momentum of your own train going, through your own starts and failure, your pushing and pulling, and then—and only then—surrender to that great electrical grid in the sky to pull your behemoth of unstoppable steel towards places you might have never imagined had you gone it alone.

- **Possible:** wait (for someone/something to move the train out of the station)
- **Impossible:** surrender (without starting)
- **Repossible:** start (the train into motion)

8

A VISION OF THE FUTURE INSTEAD OF A MEMORY OF THE PAST

WE CAN SURRENDER TO OUR PAST OR TO OUR FUTURE. IT'S OUR CHOICE.

"Ask yourself: Can I be defined by a vision of the future instead of the memories of the past?"

— Dr. Joe Dispenza

By default, we are surrendering to our past on a regular basis. Our present day consists of reworking, reliving, and repeating our past. In a way, it's all we know. We know the past because it's happened, we experienced it already. It's a known entity.

Better the devil you know than the angel you don't. Or maybe, "Better the past you know than the future you don't."

In order to arrive in our future, at least the future we're striving towards, we need to consciously live as if the future were already here. As if what will happen tomorrow happens today.

If tomorrow were here, if tomorrow were today yet the tomorrow of our dreams, how would you act? In terms of surrendering, if your dream life or future personality were here today and you were today the person of tomorrow you have been working towards, wouldn't it relieve some of the stress and effort and "trying" you're currently exuding and give you extra energy to make it truly happen?

In other words, if we can manage, even slightly, even if it's just a smidgen of a sampling of a piece of our future selves, to act as if our future self is already here, we have crossed a line already towards becoming that person.

Yes, it's a bit of "fake it 'till you make it" but those are words describing the same thing. What if we lived our future self until we became our future self? At what point does "acting" as if it already happened merge with actually already happening?

You know when you're sick or hungover or have a pain or ache? All you can think about it when it will be over. If you're smart, you'll occupy yourself with other activities than moping around moaning and groaning about how terrible the present moment is and you'll "do something else." Ideally, that something else is something you would do if you weren't hungover, sick, or in pain.

At some point, something shifts. Often, it comes along without really noticing. There usually isn't a lot of fanfare and fireworks but it's often more of a case of, "Oh, hey, wait a minute. I feel better. When did this happen?"

Ideally, we'll go ahead with our future selves (not hungover, etc.), act as if that was in the past and we'll move into our future.

Let's pick on a random stranger and choose something that hurts. Volunteers? OK, fine, me.

I'd like to be on more podcasts as a guest. "Gee, Bradley, how does that happen? Are they going to call you out of the blue or are you going to need to systematically research shows and then contact them directly?"

Yes, uh, the latter.

So what's happening?

Uh, nothing. I suppose I'm waiting around.

"Gee, Bradley, why don't read a few paragraphs back in YOUR OWN BOOK and take actions based on who you want to be in the future (someone who wants to be a guest on more podcast) and take action by contacting them (oh, I don't know, aim low, contact one per week) and keep records and make it happen.

Can you see how this "future" action will turn me into my future self? I want to be on more podcasts. I'm doing, ahem, nothing about it currently (and haven't done much about it in the past) yet I even know what to do! I have the steps, I even have a list of podcasts yet I don't contact them. #notrocketscience

The memory of the past is me not being a guest on podcasts. That memory I'm continuing to achieve (but doing nothing) so that my present is also of me not being on podcasts.

The vision of the future is being a guest on podcasts. In order to achieve that, I need to act like someone who is on podcasts. That person regularly reaches out to podcast hosts requesting a spot on their show.

Sound easy? Sound simple?

That's because it is.

Does it take a bit of effort? Yep.

Does it take a mindset shift? Oh yeah.

- **Possible:** live your present just like the past
- **Impossible:** skip the present and make the past the future
- **Repossible:** act now as if tomorrow is today

9

IT'S NOT HOPE, IT'S NOT WISHING, IT'S NOT MAYBE SOMEDAY

YOU'LL KNOW WHEN THIS SWITCHES

"Everything comes to us that belongs to us if we create the capacity to receive it."

— Rabindranath Tagore

Believe.

Remember accept? Way back there in this book? In some ways, it's very impersonal. I can quickly accept something and it doesn't sink in, it doesn't have to mean too much to me.

It's not personal.

Let's take a quick peek into our friend the dictionary for some guidance and understanding.

> ***hope:*** *to look forward to with desire and reasonable confidence.*

"Reasonable confidence" doesn't sound like a whole lot. What if the doctor said, "Yes, sir, we're going to operate on your heart and we have a reasonable confidence it will be a success."

I might be skedaddling out of that hospital.

Let's see if we have any more luck with wish.

wish: *to want; desire; long for*

OK, yep, need some of that. We need to want the thing, desire the outcome, even long for it.

It's all good but I don't feel that much closer to the outcome. I'm still a little rattled by my concern with hope...

How about our section heading here? Believe.

believe: *to have confidence in the truth, the existence, or the reliability of something, although without absolute proof that one is right in doing so*

Our confidence is no longer muddled by "reasonable." We don't have absolute truth that it's "right" but we're as close as we're going to get.

Are you ready to receive?

We can wish all day. We can hope our entire lives. We, eventually, ideally, get to believe.

Yet, there's one more step: receive.

I often hear about the "fear of success." Remember, the common phrase is "fear of failure."

Are you *ready to receive success*?

Can you honest and truly, hand on your heart, answer this in full confidence that you're ready to receive what you're asking for, wishing for, hoping for and believing in?

I am fully aware that this element of the equation is buried here in a chapter in a section of this book yet this book might as well be titled:

Are You Ready to Receive?

I feel we need a numbered list to show the hierarchy, the progression, the ascension of mindset here because it's ridiculously important. I'm going to add in a few more verbs in case you associate more clearly with some others.

1. Dream
2. Doubt
3. Fear
4. Vacillate
5. Wish
6. Hope
7. Consider
8. Pause
9. Accept
10. Trust
11. Conclude
12. Tremble
13. Believe
14. Expect
15. Admit
16. Shudder
17. Receive

How about those physical actions in there? Recognize any of those? *Tremble* as the realization comes in that, "Whoa, wait a minute here. I actually believe this is happening."

But *shudder* might be the most glorious. It's either when you bite into a lemon and that tangy, bitter and sour taste makes half of your body shudder in revolt.

Yet this *shudder* is when it's about to sink in to your belief, when you go from believing to being ready to receive, when whatever it is you're seeking is dropping into your mind, your heart, your gut and you not only believe but you feel it, you know it, it has become you.

This isn't about actually receiving—yet.

This is about being *ready* to receive.

You physically, emotionally, and physiologically shudder from the recognition that you are ready to receive, you are ready to get it, have it be delivered, you're at the door, waiting to enter, it's finally time to surrender.

- **Possible:** hope
- **Impossible:** go back to chapter one
- **Repossible:** ready to receive

PART III

SURRENDER

"Surrender is like a fish finding the current and going with it."

— Mark Nepo

10

INTRODUCTION TO SURRENDER

IT'S ABOUT TO GET REAL

"The moment of surrender is not when life is over, it's when it begins."

— Marianne Williamson

It's about to get real.

Or unreal.

Or surreal.

You choose.

There's a quote that has stuck with me over the years and once this sinks in, once you accept it and believe it you can rest with ease, peace, and confidence.

Sounds great, I know. Here you go.

"If you knew who walked beside you at all times, on the path that you have chosen, you could never experience fear or doubt again."

— Dr. Wayne Dyer

So how do you know who walks beside you? Yep, that's the ticket. There's the rub. This is the belief. This is what we're surrendering to.

Now what you interpret to be beside you is up to you. Remember the chapter on Accept? God, spirit, Tinkerbell? Yep, any one of those will do just fine–or whatever you like.

But if we have progressed from acceptance to belief then we're ready for the next step: surrender.

The Broken Arm

Back in belief, we believed our arm healed because we experienced it first hand. It was our own arm. It was broken, it healed, now it's no longer broken.

Keep in mind, unless you're a doctor or enjoy reading about biology or the human body on weekends, you're probably not going to really understand how your body healed your arm.

I mean, sure, let's take it from a layman's perspective. Proteins, blood, cartilage, and bone all form together to fix your arm. But how much bone is needed? What if it was too broken? Does it matter if you're sick or weak?

Does it matter if you don't believe your body can heal your arm?

Would it matter if you tried, with all of your cognitive power, to NOT heal your arm? What if you gave signals to your body, instructions, suggestions, dreams, intentions that said, "Body, do not heal my arm, please."

None of it matters.

Your arm is going to heal.

Your body, in its wisdom, in its DNA, will fix your arm.

Can we accept, can we believe, that there is a force, a knowing, a "something" that is behind the scenes making this happen?

Is it all just DNA and blood and cells? How does it "know" what to do? Where is the command system, the one giving the orders about what to do?

Do we have any influence on this process? Could we slow it down, speed it up? Why do some people heal more quickly than others? Some not at all?

What if we had even the tiniest influence on the functions of our body?

Here are a few little exercises for kicks.

If you think of something really sad, maybe even tragic, and let it sink in, let it get to you, you can get tears in your eyes. So, a thought you had, something that wasn't there before, not a physical thing, you didn't put onions in your eyes, caused something physical to happen in your body.

Have you ever tried imagining a lemon? Biting into it, even from the outside, like you would an apple? If you really give it your best, your taste buds are going to "taste" that lemon even though it's not there.

Last one. You're scared, nervous, maybe there's a burglar outside of your home or you have an important exam and you're waiting for the results. Your body might sweat, your heart rate might increase.

Let's Take a Step Away from the Physical

For the sake of this example and to get us over the edge, let's make it even easier.

I'm not going to say your thoughts can influence your body to the extent that you could get you could get rid of your headache or even something more drastic like heal a disease.

Nope, let's keep this simple.

Do you know if you laugh a lot, you can, sometimes, just make yourself happier? Great. Yeah, do that, it's fun.

But that's "matter moving matter." It's an action on a certain level creating an action on a similar level.

What if we went higher?

What if we could reach a level higher where we, well, to stick with he happiness thread here, guided our minds or hearts to be happier?

If we can make our foreheads sweat, why couldn't we change something as vague as our happiness? Or at least feel a little better?

- **Possible:** give
- **Impossible:** give up
- **Repossible:** give in

A video representation of surrendering is ready for your eyeballs at surrender-surrender.repossible.com.

11

WE'RE ALREADY IN OUR WORST CASE SCENARIO

IT CAN ONLY GET BETTER

"In any moment of decision, the best thing you can do is the right thing, the next best thing is the wrong thing, and the worst thing you can do is nothing."

— Theodore Roosevelt

I heard someone say this the other and it really hit home. It was one of those:

> *"Duh, gee, well, wow, yeah, that really makes sense and YES, I need to take action if I want to get out of the current scenario because I'm clearly not in the best case scenario right now or at least it could be better so, yeah, that."*

I might not have said it all quite like that but this is one of those short chapters where the title can be used as something to amaze your friends, say out loud during a lull at your dinner party.

Then you can explain it that if you don't do anything towards your best case scenario then you're already in your worst case scenario.

Another goal I have with my books, alongside reshaping humanity as we know it, trickling peace onto our planet, and spreading so much love that hate just has no place to go, is giving you witty phrases you can use at parties or at your kids' basketball game when it's halftime and you don't really know the other parents so well and you're feeling like saying something and the weather has been taken care of and you can just come out and say it:

"We're already in our worst case scenario."

See? And you thought this book was only going to introduce you to spirit angels, transform your mind, and alter your personality. These are the secret bonuses you get for digging deep into this book.

OK, fine, it can get worse, too, but not again and again. Not if we keep at it, know our direction, and share our journey with others and hold their hands to move onward and upward.

We're better together.

We're already in our worst case scenario.

Ready to try?

Turn the page.

- **Possible:** do nothing
- **Impossible:** the worst happens (again and again)
- **Repossible:** what's the worst that can happen?

12

TRY

DIDN'T YODA HAVE SOMETHING TO SAY ABOUT TRYING?

> "I can accept failure, everyone fails at something. But I can't accept not trying."
>
> — Michael Jordan

I'm pretty sure it was Yoda who said something about there not being any "try" but there is only "do."

Yep, I get it.

You can "try" to surrender to whatever it is here we're surrendering to or you can just "do" it.

Ha, I'm a little slow sometimes but I just put together that I have Michael Jordan and then "just do it" here on the same page.

But I want to give you an out, an "excuse," a second chance.

Here we are deep into this book called Surrender. Hopefully, this far along, you have accepted and believed yet this last bit, this one big hurdle might have you stumped.

You accept it's possible.

You believe it's possible for you.

Yet this third leg of the race just isn't cutting it for you.

Sure, Yoda says do.

Nike says just do it.

But that's a blob of goo and a brand.

What about this person, yeah, you, sitting in your secret hideaway, listening to guided meditations every morning and you're just not getting to that whole surrender level where, oh, I don't know, the ground is removed from beneath you, the universe goes black and ***you're OK with it.***

That's how it goes for me.

I'm in my chair, even in my meditation physically there sitting in a chair, but then I'm seeing myself sitting in my meditation and the ground goes out from under me, to the left and right disappears, above was already dark and nothing and there I am, just me and the, whatever, the universe.

If you'd like, I can walk you though this. Here we go: surrendertry.repossible.com.

- **Possible:** do
- **Impossible:** completely believe a gooey blob character in a movie
- **Repossible:** try

13

RISE UP (INSTEAD OF FALLING DOWN)

PULL OTHERS WITH US

"A rising tide lifts all boats."

— John F. Kennedy

Although this is along the lines of the chapter called "A Vision of the Future Instead of a Memory of the Past," it's not exactly the same thing.

They're on different planes.

Future is forward and past is backward whereas this chapter is more up and down. While we're talking directions, left and right are still open and can add then your own personal touch or flavor to where you're heading.

But we want to go up, improve, get better or even strive towards heights we haven't ever reached before.

Perhaps Surrender is understood as rising up or positive but I wanted to to drive the point home that surrendering is going to head in that direction naturally.

Let's take it one more little level higher though, shall we?

As I write this, we're in the middle of the Corona pandemic. I'm originally from California where you could then add fires, distance learning for most all students in the state, heat waves, power outages, protests about race and police.

It's going to sound like a live in a bubble or even that I would like to live in a bubble and I'm not even going to deny that this book, Surrender, together with a previous book in the Repossible series, Meditate, are bubbles in a way.

We are escaping from the day to day to gather our thoughts, achieve clarity, and sharpen our focus.

> *If I brought all of the mayhem into my meditations, I wouldn't be able to surrender to much at all because I would probably be overwhelmed with everything that's going on in the world.*

So yes, in that sense, meditation and surrendering are escapes. But then when we're done with a meditation session (in which hopefully surrendered to some extent), we're going to be right back in that real world with all of its challenges.

I wholeheartedly believe that surrendering to our own higher power during meditation (and, ideally, throughout as much of the rest of the day as possible) is a way to make the world as a whole a better place.

If we can rise up, if we can reach up to our own higher powers and become that "better" person on a daily basis, aren't we then adding to the uplifting of the population as a whole?

It's much like the oxygen mask dropping from the airplane and how you're supposed to put it over your own mouth before you care for your child sitting next to you.

If you first gave the oxygen to the child and you died, that child wouldn't know how (depending on their age, of course) to take care of you. So by saving yourself first, by lifting your own self up first, and then taking care of others, we are stronger for it.

Also, by lifting up others, we empower our own lifting, we strengthen our own ascent so we are better equipped to do it again, over and over, for others, for more and more people and we'll get better and better at it, we'll become more efficient and effective.

So although it might seem obvious that we want to "surrender up" and not down, there are many reasons to consciously remember we are heading up.

As we rise up, we bring others with us.

They'll rooting for us, they're depending on us, they're waiting for us.

- **Possible:** surrender
- **Impossible:** surrender down
- **Repossible:** surrender up

14

MATTER TO MATTER, ENERGY TO MATTER, AND REMEMBERING PIN CODE AT THE BANK

IT'S ALL THERE. IT'S JUST A MATTER OF ACCESS.

"Once we accept our limits, we go beyond them."

— Albert Einstein

Your "higher self" explained in the simplest of terms we can all understand.

Here in this book called Surrender, we're talking about giving in to a higher power. Yet for those of us who haven't quite been able to put a finger on what that really means or what it looks like, I'm going to shower you with examples.

Here's one of my favorites.

You're at the ATM, the abbreviation for what they call in the United States the Automated Teller Machine or the bank machine. It's where you put in your bank card, your secret pin code or numbered password, and you withdraw cash.

Remember I used to go to Las Vegas quite a bit as a kid and so I remember what it was like to see money pour out a machine. This new-fangled ATM invention was awesome: you were always a winner!

Years later, I realized it was your own money you were withdrawing. **Much less fun.**

But I digress.

Conscious and Unconscious Mind (and Memory)

The important thing about this ATM is you need two things, well, three things:

1. A bank card
2. A PIN code (password) and, ideally,
3. Money in the bank to withdraw.

If you don't have all three, you're not going to get very far.

#1 and #3 are physical items. You need the actual card to physically insert into the machine and the money, the dollars, the euros, need to be in the bank to get them out.

It's that #2 that can be tricky sometimes.

Even if your pin code is part of your zip code (not recommended), the year of your birth (probably the worst pin code), or the month and day of your birthday (really, you still do this?) and you use it on a regular basis, there are moments when we just can't remember it.

Here's what often happens.

You're standing there in front of the machine and if there are people behind you (external pressure, forces beyond your control), it can make you a little nervous because they also want to get to the ATM and they're in a hurry. Added pressure.

You insert your card and all of the sudden, your mind goes blank.

These are a series of four numbers you might type in on a weekly basis. If you're like most of us, you haven't changed these four numbers in years–if ever. In fact, you probably don't even know how to change them (I admit, as techy and password cautious as I am, I don't know how to change my bank pin nor, even worse, have I even tried).

We have these four numbers embedded in our minds, almost

branded into the back side of our forehead to the point where we don't even need to *think* (remember this verb, it's important for later) about what the pin code it, *we just know it*.

Yet there we are, we haven't changed the numbers in years and for some reason, we can remember them on this particular occasion.

Matter to Matter

It's been so long without a numbered list, it's time for a list of verbs. Here's what you're going to do next.

1. Try to remember
2. Try harder to dig through your memory
3. Doubt yourself
4. (Psychologically) kick yourself because this is silly, right? You *know* this.
5. Try some more
6. Probe
7. Push
8. Look behind you (are the other people getting antsy?)
9. Laugh (because this is ridiculous)
10. Worry (your brain is going, your memory isn't what it used to be)
11. Breathe. You've got this. You know this.
12. Ask why it's not coming back.
13. Try again
14. Put your fingers onto the keyboard and often:
15. Close your eyes (this occasionally works)
16. Purse your lips
17. Curse quietly, increase heart rate, cancel the transaction, and walk away.

Ever had one of those? Some of those? All of those? It's so common, it happens to the best of us. Wait, it happens to all of us.

What happens next is the good part, the part that's often hard to understand yet, remember, we're in a book called Surrender, the part we want to get better at, the "transaction" we want to practice and make the goal.

Energy to Matter

You take a few steps away from the ATM. You probably glance at the people still in line and maybe you shrug your shoulders or say something as an excuse. Well, if they even noticed you couldn't remember your pin.

You take a few more steps.

You doubt your memory.

You might even worry slightly about your sanity, your brain. Maybe you had a mini stroke. Maybe you're older than you think. Maybe you're losing it. Maybe you had too much to drink last night. Maybe this, maybe that. You're doubting.

Often what happens next is yet another external factor comes into play. Since you're so focused on your memory and your pin code, you're not paying attention to your surroundings. Maybe a bicyclist flies by and almost hits you. Maybe you walk into the street and a car zooms by. Or you just take steps away from the ATM keep trying to remember.

At some point, usually only in a matter of seconds, your concentration, your focus, your awareness goes from the ATM, from the pin code to something else, anything else.

Where were you heading next? To the supermarket? To a friend's house? Home?

Your thoughts veer away from the pin code finally.

Then, all of the sudden, without having expected it, without trying for it, and without focusing on it, the pin code comes to you. Depending on how you best get your information, it will come to you in different ways.

It could come to you as a visual where you see the numbers on the number pad and you see your fingers moving over the numbers and pressing them in the correct order. Or maybe you hear the numbers, maybe in your own voice, come to you. Or you see the numbers in front of your mind. Or you just feel it and you know them again.

Of course, you always knew them. There were always there.

But now they're back.

Often, hopefully, you'll smile, you might laugh a little at yourself. One to not do is to get mad at yourself, frustrated or angry or sad or worried.

Your subconscious just gave you the answer. This is what we wanted, right? The pin code. Yet how we got it is key.

Remember back when we were trying so hard? We were pushing and prodding, frustrated and anxious. It didn't come to us. Even if we had stayed in front of the machine for another 10 minutes, it probably wouldn't have come to us. Maybe 10 hours.

Yet in a span of something more along the lines of 10 seconds, we had it. Boom, just like that.

Matter to matter versus energy to matter.

The "matter" is on a certain level. Say, trying or using our conscious memory to try to make it happen. We're using what we know to get an answer.

When we take the steps away from the ATM, we are giving up, we're giving in (to that higher power) and we're getting out of the way–we're getting out of our own way.

Then it happens. What we had been trying to so hard to achieve, what we wanted, where we had focused our energy, it didn't go away. We know we still want to know the ATM pin code. We also know that we know the answer.

But we're in our own way.

We then surrender to a greater power, a power, a knowing that is already in our own selves, to get the answer.

We then get the answer with less effort (in fact, usually zero effort), less time, and in an unexpected way–or even to the point where we thought we gave up on "trying" to get the answer and we were moving on.

This is surrender.

This is the simplest, most real-life-situation example I have come across to illustrate how surrendering works in our lives.

This was a pin code. Four numbers. An "easy" one.

What if we follow the same process with other answers or goals or desires in our lives?

What if we wanted not to know just our pin code but what chapter we should write in our book? Maybe what job we should take? What to say to that girl you met yesterday? How to buy the house you wanted? How to heal your wounded or infected or diseased body?

This list is a tiny one.

Surrendering is the key to getting the answers in a different way, through some simple–but not always easy–steps that we can learn to improve in.

Let this chapter sit with you.

Try, push, prod, make an effort. Know what it is you want, what' your'e after, make it clear.

Walk away, take your mind off of it.

Surrender to the answer.

I did my "Forgot My PIN Code" act for my Toastmasters group on video: surrender-pin.repossible.com.

- **Possible:** think harder, wait
- **Impossible:** push, prod, plead
- **Repossible:** let it drop in

PART IV

BEHIND THE SCENES

A LOOK INTO THE CREATION OF THIS BOOK

15

UNDER THE HOOD

OR IS THIS THE SAUSAGE FACTORY? THE PART YOU DON'T REALLY WANT TO SEE?

"I love more than anything looking at a movie scene by scene and seeing the intention behind it. It allows you to really appreciate the hand of the filmmaker."

— Jodie Foster

As the Repossible series progresses, I'm getting more and more questions about how it's built, what's the energy source behind it and, "Bradley, how can you keep all of these ideas and books and plans straight."

I'm going to pull back the curtain here and share a bit of my process.

I like using the words "I'm" and "process" in the same sentence because it's a bit of an internal joke in that I don't really have a process that I know of yet that's just it: it's a process I don't know of consciously.

So much of what I create comes through meditation and then, ahem, surrendering to a higher field of knowledge and wisdom and **I'm just the messenger.**

In the following chapters, I'll take you through some of the exercises I do to build out a topic, screen it, filter it, and sift out the silt and get down to the shiny flakes of gold.

- **Possible:** keep quietly churning out the product on the assembly line
- **Impossible:** keep "process" secrets
- **Repossible:** share the factory floor mess

16

ACRONYM CHALLENGE: S.U.R.R.E.N.D.E.R.

THERE MUST BE AT LEAST 3 "R'S" IN THERE...

"Creativity is just connecting things. When you ask creative people how they did something, they feel a little guilty because they didn't really do it, they just saw something. It seemed obvious to them after a while. That's because they were able to connect experiences they've had and synthesize new things."

— STEVE JOBS

Acronyms don't usually just magically appear. They are more something that needs some love, some work, some time.

For the past few books, I've been doing an "Acronym Challenge" for my books. Yep, Surrender has lots of letters and even one three times but still, I thought it through, I found websites that have lists of verbs and, lo and behold, it works.

As with most challenges, they shake things up, they rattle your sleepy noggin and wake you up with ideas you probably didn't think of—and maybe never would have.

Below, I even was conscious not to repeat the same "R" verbs and also tried to use the progression of how I envision the process of surrendering into #1, #2 and #3 use of the letter.

This is also an exercise we have in our "Boost your Brand with a Book" workshop to get authors thinking about their topic in new ways.

S

1. Sail
2. Scale
3. **Scream**
4. **Search**
5. Secure
6. **Seed**
7. **Seem**
8. Seize
9. Select
10. Serve
11. **Shake**
12. Shape
13. Share
14. Shine
15. **Shout**
16. **Sing**
17. **Soar**
18. Solve
19. Sort
20. Sound (out)
21. **Sow**
22. **Spark**
23. Split
24. Spring
25. Stand
26. **Start**
27. Stay
28. **Steady**

29. **Step**
30. **Stop**
31. Strike
32. **Strive**
33. Succeed
34. Support
35. **Surpass**
36. **Surprise**
37. **Surrender**
38. Surround
39. Survey
40. **Survive**

U

1. **Unbind**
2. **Unbox**
3. Unbuckle
4. **Uncork**
5. **Uncouple**
6. **Uncover**
7. **Underestimate**
8. Underline
9. **Underrate**
10. **Understand**
11. Understudy
12. Undertake
13. **Undervalue**
14. Underwrite
15. **Undo**
16. Unearth
17. Unfasten
18. **Unfold**
19. Unify
20. **Unite**

21. Unlearn
22. Unleash
23. Unload
24. Unmask
25. Unmuzzle
26. Unpack
27. Unplug
28. Unravel
29. Untangle
30. Untie
31. Unveil
32. Uproot
33. Urge
34. Utilize

R

1. Raise
2. Reach
3. React
4. Read
5. Realize
6. Reason
7. Reassure
8. Recite
9. Reckon
10. Recognize
11. Reduce
12. Refer
13. Reflect
14. Relax
15. Remember
16. Repeat
17. Request
18. Retry

19. **Return**
20. **Reveal**
21. **Review**
22. **Rid**

R

1. **Rebel**
2. **Rebound**
3. **Rebuild**
4. **Recap**
5. **Recharge**
6. **Reconsider**
7. **Recruit**
8. **Recycle**
9. **Rediscover**
10. **Redo**
11. **Refill**
12. **Regret**
13. **Rehearse**
14. **Renounce**
15. **Rescue**
16. **Respond**
17. **Reunite**
18. **Revise**
19. **Roar**
20. **Rouse**

E

1. **Ease**
2. Echo
3. Eclipse
4. Edge
5. **Educate**

6. Elaborate
7. **Elevate**
8. **Embellish**
9. **Embody**
10. **Embolden**
11. **Embrace**
12. **Emerge**
13. Emit
14. **Empower**
15. **Enable**
16. End
17. Engage
18. **Enhance**
19. **Enlighten**
20. **Enlist**
21. Enrage
22. **Enrich**
23. **Enter**
24. Entice
25. Entitle
26. **Entrust**
27. Envelop
28. **Envisage**
29. Envy
30. Equip
31. Err
32. Erupt
33. **Escape**
34. **Establish**
35. Evoke
36. **Evolve**
37. Examine
38. **Excavate**
39. **Exceed**
40. **Excel**

41. **Excite**
42. Exercise
43. **Exhale**
44. **Expand**
45. **Explore**
46. **Extend**
47. Extract
48. Exude
49. Eye

N

1. Name
2. **Narrate**
3. **Narrow**
4. **Navigate**
5. Need
6. **Negotiate**
7. Nest
8. **Nestle**
9. **Nod**
10. **Nominate**
11. **Normalize**
12. Notice
13. Notify
14. **Nourish**
15. **Nurse**

D

1. Dabble
2. **Dance**
3. Dangle
4. **Daydream**
5. **Dazzle**

6. **Deal**
7. **Decide**
8. **Declare**
9. **Decode**
10. **Dedicate**
11. Deduce
12. Deduct
13. **Deepen**
14. Defend
15. Defer
16. Define
17. **Defy**
18. Delegate
19. **Delight**
20. **Deliver**
21. **Demystify**
22. Deny
23. Depart
24. Depend
25. **Deploy**
26. Deposit
27. **Desire**
28. Determine
29. **Develop**
30. Devise
31. **Devote**
32. **Devour**
33. Diagnose
34. Dial
35. Differentiate
36. Diffuse
37. **Dig**
38. **Dip**
39. **Discard**
40. Disclose

41. Discount
42. **Discover**
43. Discuss
44. **Disembark**
45. Disguise
46. Dismiss
47. Dispatch
48. Display
49. Dispute
50. Distill
51. Distinguish
52. **Distribute**
53. Dive
54. Diversify
55. Divide
56. Do
57. Dot
58. Double
59. Dramatize
60. Draw
61. **Dream**
62. Drift
63. Drill
64. Drip
65. **Drive**
66. Dwell

E

1. Ease
2. **Echo**
3. Eclipse
4. Edge
5. **Educate**
6. **Elaborate**

7. **Elevate**
8. Embellish
9. Embody
10. Embolden
11. Embrace
12. Emerge
13. Emit
14. **Empower**
15. Enable
16. End
17. **Engage**
18. Enhance
19. Enlighten
20. Enlist
21. Enrage
22. Enrich
23. Enter
24. Entice
25. Entitle
26. Entrust
27. Envelop
28. Envisage
29. Envy
30. Equip
31. Err
32. **Erupt**
33. **Escape**
34. Establish
35. Evoke
36. Evolve
37. Examine
38. Excavate
39. Exceed
40. Excel
41. Excite

42. Exercise
43. Exhale
44. Expand
45. **Explore**
46. Extend
47. Extract
48. Exude
49. Eye

R

1. Race
2. **Radiate**
3. **Rave**
4. **Reap**
5. **Receive**
6. **Recreate**
7. Redeem
8. Refresh
9. **Refuse**
10. **Reign**
11. **Rejoice**
12. **Relate**
13. Relay
14. **Release**
15. **Relieve**
16. **Relish**
17. Reload
18. Remedy
19. **Renew**
20. **Repair**
21. Require
22. **Reset**
23. Resolve
24. Restore

25. Resuscitate
26. **Revere**
27. **Revitalize**
28. **Revive**
29. **Reward**
30. **Ride**
31. **Romp**
32. Root
33. **Rule**
34. Rustle

- **Possible:** probably get the idea of your book
- **Impossible:** hope it all comes out perfectly
- **Repossible:** do stuff that results in other stuff

17

5-WORD HOOKS: SURRENDER

NOT 4, NOT 6. 5.

"I often speak publicly, and when I do, I also get to listen to other presenters. The most memorable are the ones that hit an emotional chord with a tight story and a punch line. No fluff. Keep it creative and concise. Greatness exists in quality, not quantity."

— Lewis Howes

I got this exercise from a fellow author, Brian Meeks, although I think he used 6 words. I've done "5-Word Hooks" for my past several books and it helps me dig deeper and find exactly the right words for the right direction.

The hard part is to only use 5 words to describe your topic. It might be a list of words but if you can string together a little sentence or thought about what you're after, it can reap wonders.

Here we go for Surrender.

1. Give in to the unknown
2. Release yourself to the divine
3. You are also the divine

4. Just enough to let go.
5. Accept, Believe, (and then) Surrender
6. What is possible for you?
7. If you knew how close
8. It's right here inside you
9. Surprisingly it's
10. Close your eyes to see
11. Close your eyes to believe
12. See it when you believe
13. **Soar into the delicious unknown**
14. Let the energy take you
15. Let the force take you
16. Let the wind take you
17. Let the gust take you
18. Let the ____ take you
19. Unbox what's trapped in you
20. Unleash what's locked in you
21. So much, so close by
22. Surprise yourself, close your eyes
23. Uncork the pressure in you
24. Unite with the greater you
25. **Unite with your greater self**
26. Unmask your ...
27. Unplug from your past self
28. Give in, don't give up
29. Unveil the power within you
30. Unmask the power within you
31. **Reach for a higher self**
32. Recognize you as much more
33. Reduce your reliance on history
34. Relax, Request, Reveal, Revel, Roar
35. Relax, Request, Reveal, Revel, Roar
36. There's a greater self nearby
37. Rediscover your own true self
38. **Reunite, Recharge, Release, Reward, Rule**

- **Possible:** 12 words
- **Impossible:** 0 words
- **Repossible:** 5 words

AFTERWORD

> "Only those who will risk going too far can possibly find out how far one can go."
>
> — T. S. Eliot

I probably shouldn't do this but I'm going to share with you my favorite chapters of this book.

The odd thing is: they're not, technically, chapters.

In the Introduction, I hope, no, I wish, no, I believe that there is more to this than words on a page. Join me, join us, join Repossible at surrender.repossible.com. If you don't like it there, no harm, no foul, you can sneak away as quietly as you arrived.

Then in the Foreword, which is supposed to be written by someone else, I opt in to an alter persona, Mr. Brad Lee, and I let it all out and tell a story about what was, apparently, a turning point in my life. A point when I realized I could become a person who did a thing like that.

I'll probably "get in trouble" for writing about angry people in the chapter about yelling and screaming but those are the people I most want to reach.

In Try, I'm not just going to tell you but I'm going to show you, lead you, guide you through a meditation, yep, an actual audio file of me talking you through giving surrender a try. If readers say I didn't give any practical tips or advice in this book, they skipped this chapter—or didn't download the audio file. I'm risking, daring, and putting it all on the line by recording a guided meditation and sharing it with you. Ask me if I thought I would EVER do that a few years ago. This is surrendering in action. I'm surrendering to the crazy idea that I might be able to lead you to a higher self. Crazy, I know.

This is a risky book for me. When I started out as a writer, I thought I would write manuals for building WordPress sites (kill me now...).

Here's my ask for this afterword.

1. If this book resonated with you in any positive way, **please leave a review** on the site where you purchased this book.
2. If this book just didn't cut it or we didn't connect here or I lost you when the floor dropped out from under us in the guided meditation, don't tell a friend, don't post a negative review, **let me know**. If you sign up at surrender.repossible.com, you'll get an email from me and you can just reply. My email is in there. I'd love to hear what was missing, how I can improve it, or maybe you'd just rather hear about WordPress sites. ;-)

But mostly here, I want to thank you. Speaking of which, sounds like it's time for acknowledgements.

- **Possible:** think twice about this book
- **Impossible:** put this book down and never think of it again
- **Repossible:** share what's missing here with me, share what's working here with a friend

ACKNOWLEDGMENTS

> "As we express our gratitude, we must never forget that the highest appreciation is not to utter words, but to live by them."
>
> — John F. Kennedy

At least as of this version, I dedicated this book to Joe Dispenza. Had he not been such the numbers guy, the scientist, the "I'm going to back up all of this woo woo with science," I probably never would have, well, surrendered to the level on which I live today.

But I mostly want to acknowledge you.

You are the type of person who reads all the way to the end. You want change, you see it before you and you know you'll get there. You vacuum up all information, digest it into knowledge, put it into practice, and reap the results.

Whether those results are at the level you're "happy" with is a question of mindset but that sounds like yet another book.

I want to thank you for reading this book—and any others you've read in the Repossible series.

I write books that I want to read. Books that I wish I had read a few short years ago. Although, if you seen me on camera, you'll think I'm a happy-go-lucky dude who's life is a walk in the park. Yep, I am.

But I absolutely, positively, and way, way unfortunately haven't always been this giddy.

I write the books I wanted to read a few short years ago in order to take me to "the next level" in happiness, joy, meaning, purpose, clarity, you-get-the-idea and I'm thankful that you're reading this now as I hope I can catapult you faster, more efficiently and more effectively, towards the dream you're after.

I write for me.

I write for you.

As I write this, I can't not think about my mom, who recently passed away. She helped so many people. She was a middle-school teacher and she received notes, up to her dying day, about shy 7th graders who said things like, "Mrs. Charbonneau, you changed my life." "Mrs. Charbonneau, you probably never noticed me, I was the quiet girl in the back, but you gave me the confidence to believe in myself and I went on to high school and I was the first one in my family to go to college thanks to you."

I have some big shoes to fill!

But that's all I want. I want to help people get what they want, realize their dreams, find their passion, live their purpose.

By reading this book, you acknowledge me and I take this moment to acknowledge you.

Thank you for being here. Thank you for reading. Thank you for being you.

I'm rooting for you.

- **Possible:** thank people who got me here
- **Impossible:** go it alone
- **Repossible:** thank you

ABOUT THE AUTHOR

"Surrender is for wimps!"

"I don't need anyone's help!"

"I've got this."

"I'm a solo superstar."

"I'm doing fine."

"I mean, right?"

"Hello?"

"Echo! Echo!"

There you have it. I could put a little timeline next to the list above over the past years.

But that would be too depressing.

I used to be very stubborn (or *determined*, depending on how you like to spin it) and *proud*, even fiercely proud, of how *independent* I was, how I could do it all myself, and how I was the best person for the job.

So what changed?

This is going to sound a little weird but: it just wasn't any fun.

Don't get me wrong, I still wholeheartedly believe we CAN go it alone, we WILL be fine, and we'll eventually GET there.

But why bother?

Going it alone is slower, harder, and solitary.

> "Wait a minute, Mr. Bradley. I thought we were surrendering to our own greater self (or whatever). Aren't we still alone?"
>
> — Maybe You

This is going to take a bit of a stretch of imagination but no, I think when we surrender to our greater self we are no longer really alone.

Take that for what you may but by inviting in a higher power we are allowing not just that ascended level of our own selves but by opening the door, we allow others, yes, other people, also to come on in and join the party.

We're deliciously getting close to book #10: Play. Just a little teaser, OK fine, it's a whopper of a teaser, but Play is what we're really, really after here.

Everything leads to Play.

Elevate, book #11, will bring us to the next level up so we can do it all again in our "next life" (which is actually still this life—unless you're a cat) but Play is the finish line.

> "Uh, Bradley, aren't we still in the Surrender book here?"
>
> — You (checking in on me)

Yep and yes, we can do it alone. But surrendering is the easiest, fastest, and most fun way to get there.

I'm a recovering solopreneur. I wanted to go it alone for years if not decades.

I write this "About the Author" section to try, to plead, to get down on my knees and implore you to surrender to a greater force.

The easy part?

That greater force is still you.

If one book in the Repossible Series is both the easiest and the hardest, it's Surrender.

I've done it. I was stubborn, patient, and clueless.

If you're any of those, take my hand and let me introduce you to the Bradley Charbonneau who has taken things to a higher level and has found there is more than self, there is greater than solo, there is you and then there is Super Natural You.

Nice to meet you.

Whew. Now that I got that out of the way, here's that regular *about the author* stuff.

I currently live in a little town outside of Utrecht in The Netherlands with my wife Saskia, famous two young boys of "The Adventures of Li & Lu" fame, and our at-least-as-famous dog Pepper.

This is my twenty-sixth book.

It is far, far, far, like oh-so-far from my last.

Find, ask, discuss, play, dare, and surrender at:
bradleycharbonneau.com

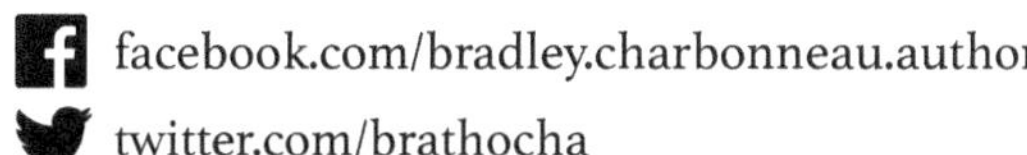

facebook.com/bradley.charbonneau.author
twitter.com/brathocha

instagram.com/brathocha

ALSO BY BRADLEY CHARBONNEAU

Most of my books are also available as audiobooks (which I giddily narrate). Search for my name at your favorite audiobook distributor, slip on your headphones, and let me take you away.

Repossible

Repossible

Every Single Day (+ Playbook)

Ask

Dare

Create

Decide

Meditate

Spark

Surrender

Play

Elevate

Frequency

Every Single Day

Every Single Day Playbook

Every Single Day Kids

Every Single Day Teens (I want to write this one because I want to read this one...)

Charlie Holiday

Now Is Your Chance (1)

Second Chance (2)

Chance of a Lifetime (3)

For Creatives

Audio for Authors

Meditation for Creatives (2021)

Shorts

Secret Bus to Paradise

Where I (Already) Am

Pass the Sour Cream

A Trip to Hel

Drive-By Dropping

Li & Lu

The Secret of Kite Hill (1)

The Secret of Markree Castle (2)

The Key to Markree Castle (3)

The Gift of Markree Castle (4)

Driehoek (5)

Really Old ...

urban travel guide SAN FRANCISCO

THE END

It takes more effort to fight it.

Surrender.

www.ingramcontent.com/pod-product-compliance
Lightning Source LLC
LaVergne TN
LVHW010934110826
845149LV00013B/2601

* 9 7 8 1 3 9 3 2 1 7 7 6 3 *